Baghdad

by Betsy Rathburn

Illustrated by Diego Vaisberg

BLASTOFF! MISSIONS

BELLWETHER MEDIA
MINNEAPOLIS, MN

Blastoff! Missions takes you on a learning adventure! Colorful illustrations and exciting narratives highlight cool facts about our world and beyond. Read the mission goals and follow the narrative to gain knowledge, build reading skills, and have fun!

Traditional Nonfiction

Narrative Nonfiction

Blastoff! Universe

MISSION GOALS

> FIND YOUR SIGHT WORDS IN THE BOOK.

> LEARN ABOUT DIFFERENT TIMES IN BAGHDAD'S HISTORY.

> LEARN ABOUT THE DIFFERENT PEOPLE OR GROUPS WHO HAVE CONTROLLED BAGHDAD.

This edition first published in 2024 by Bellwether Media, Inc.

No part of this publication may be reproduced in whole or in part without written permission of the publisher. For information regarding permission, write to Bellwether Media, Inc., Attention: Permissions Department, 6012 Blue Circle Drive, Minnetonka, MN 55343.

Library of Congress Cataloging-in-Publication Data

LC record for Baghdad available at: https://lccn.loc.gov/2023044971

Editor: Christina Leaf   Designer: Andrea Schneider

Printed in the United States of America, North Mankato, MN.

This is **Blastoff Jimmy**! He is here to help you on your mission and share fun facts along the way!

Table of Contents

Welcome to Baghdad!

Baghdad, Iraq, is full of activity! Cars fill the city streets. People shop at markets and work downtown. Let's go back in time to explore this busy capital city's history!

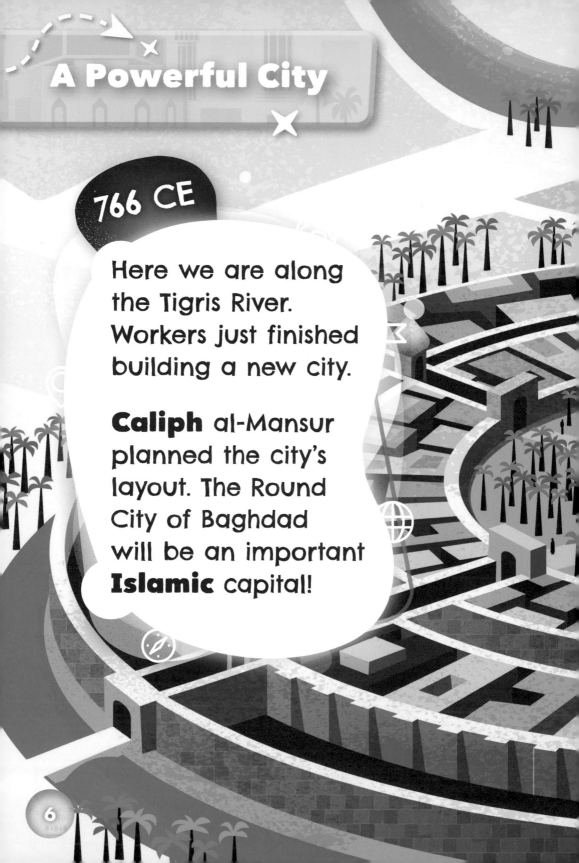

A Powerful City

766 CE

Here we are along the Tigris River. Workers just finished building a new city.

Caliph al-Mansur planned the city's layout. The Round City of Baghdad will be an important **Islamic** capital!

Tigris River

Round City
of Baghdad

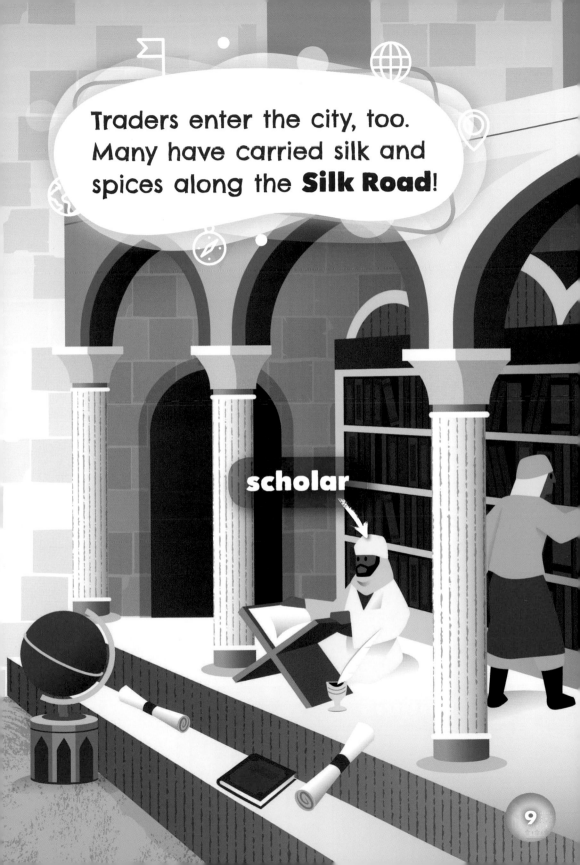

1258

Baghdad has fallen. **Mongols** have taken the city.

The famous library, the House of Wisdom, burns. The **invaders** throw its books into the river. Will Baghdad ever recover?

Mongols

▶ JIMMY SAYS ◀

The House of Wisdom stood for hundreds of years. It held many thousands of books!

mid-1500s

The **Ottomans** now control Baghdad. The city is losing strength. Still, many people live here.

Ottoman

People gather in this street.
They buy books in the market!

A Fight for Power

jets

1980

Baghdad is under attack. Bombs dropped by Iranian jets rock the city.

Saddam Hussein leads Iraq. He seeks more control over the area. Many fear what the future may bring.

soldier

tank

2003

United States soldiers and tanks fill Baghdad. They want to stop Saddam Hussein.

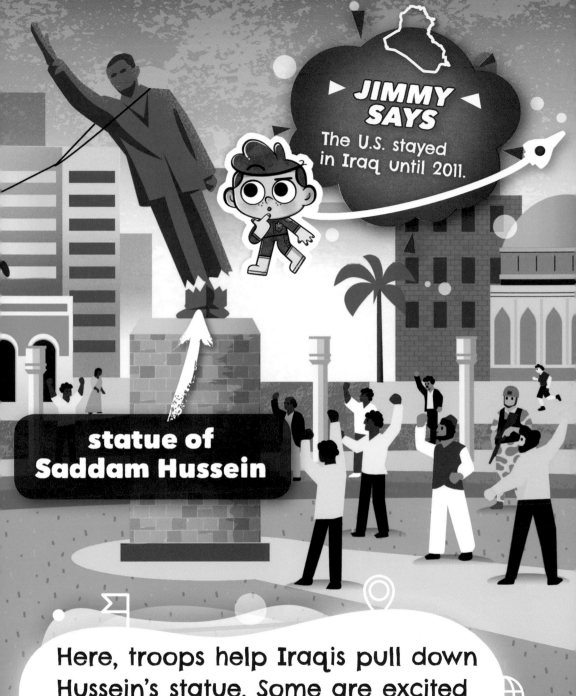

JIMMY SAYS
The U.S. stayed in Iraq until 2011.

statue of Saddam Hussein

Here, troops help Iraqis pull down Hussein's statue. Some are excited about the changes. Others worry about the future.

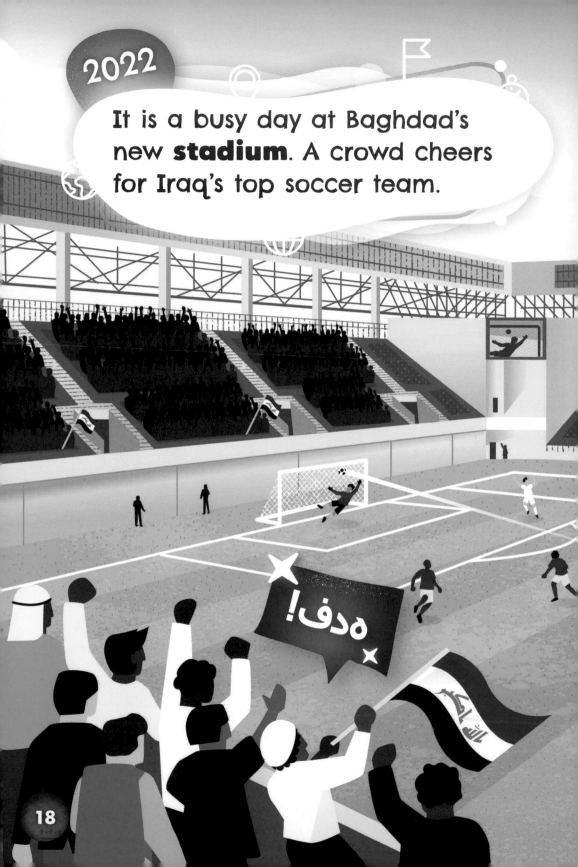

The team will score many goals here. Iraqis love to root for their teams!

stadium

mosque

today

Visitors can explore Baghdad's past in **mosques** and museums. This city has gone through hard times. But its people are proud to call Baghdad home!

Baghdad Timeline

766 CE: The Round City of Baghdad is finished four years after it was founded

800s: Many scholars fill Baghdad during a period of science and learning

1258: Baghdad falls to Mongol invaders

1534: The Ottomans begin a long period of rule in Baghdad

1980: Iran bombs Baghdad early in the Iran-Iraq War

2003: U.S. soldiers reach Baghdad during the U.S. invasion of Iraq

2022: The Al-Zawraa Stadium is completed

Baghdad, Iraq

Glossary

caliph–a Muslim leader

invaders–people who come from one place to take over another place

Islamic–related to Islam; Islam is a religion in which people follow the teachings of the Prophet Muhammad as told to him by Allah.

Mongols–members of an ancient nomadic group of people in Asia known for being fierce warriors; people with Mongol backgrounds now live mostly in Mongolia, China, and Russia.

mosques–buildings that Muslims use for worship

Ottomans–members of the Ottoman Empire; the Ottoman Empire was a large empire that controlled parts of Europe, Asia, and North Africa.

scholars–people who are very educated and often study a particular subject

Silk Road–a large network of trade routes that connected Europe and Asia

stadium–a big building that hosts large sports games, concerts, and other events

To Learn More

AT THE LIBRARY

Gould, Sloane. *Iraq*. 2nd ed. Buffalo, N.Y.: Cavendish Square Publishing, 2024.

Laird, Elizabeth. *A Fistful of Pearls and Other Tales from Iraq*. London, U.K.: Frances Lincoln Children's Books, 2008.

Sabelko, Rebecca. *Iraq*. Minneapolis, Minn.: Bellwether Media, 2023.

ON THE WEB

FACTSURFER

Factsurfer.com gives you a safe, fun way to find more information.

1. Go to www.factsurfer.com.

2. Enter "Baghdad" into the search box and click 🔍.

3. Select your book cover to see a list of related content.

BEYOND THE MISSION

> WHICH PART OF BAGHDAD'S HISTORY WOULD YOU LIKE TO VISIT? WHY?

> WHAT WOULD YOU STUDY IN BAGHDAD'S HOUSE OF WISDOM?

> WHAT DO YOU THINK BAGHDAD'S FUTURE WILL BE LIKE?

Index